INSIDE MARTIAL ARTS

AIKIDO

合気道

合気道

合気道

by Alex Monnig

Content Consultant:
Tristan Chermack, head instructor Spirit Aikido, Eden Prairie, MN
Member of the Mid America Aikido Federation

SportsZone
An Imprint of Abdo Publishing | www.abdopublishing.com

www.abdopublishing.com

Published by Abdo Publishing, a division of ABDO, PO Box 398166, Minneapolis, Minnesota 55439. Copyright © 2015 by Abdo Consulting Group, Inc. International copyrights reserved in all countries. No part of this book may be reproduced in any form without written permission from the publisher. SportsZone™ is a trademark and logo of Abdo Publishing.

Printed in the United States of America, North Mankato, Minnesota
102014
012015

THIS BOOK CONTAINS
RECYCLED MATERIALS

Cover Photo: Shutterstock Images
Interior Photos: Shutterstock Images, 1, 4–5, 10–11, 21 (top); Achim Scheidemann/EPA/Newscom, 9; LifesizeImages/iStockphoto, 12, 22–23, 26; Stéphane Ouzounoff/Photononstop, 15, 32–33; Guo Yong/Xinhua Press/Corbis, 17; Ren Zhenglai/Xinhua Press/Corbis, 18, 21 (bottom); Ren Zhenglai/Xinhua/Photoshot/Newscom, 20 (top); Everett Kennedy Brown/EPA/Newscom, 20 (bottom); Marsha Halper/KRT/Newscom, 24, 36; Aping Vision/STS/Ocean/Corbis, 27, 29, 30; Wang Lili/Xinhua Press/Corbis, 35; Andrew Shlykoff/Alamy, 37; Wang Lili/Xinhua/Photoshot/Newscom, 38; iStockphoto, 39; Dimitri Iundt/TempSport/Corbis, 40–41; Sysoeva Lyubov/Itar-Tass Photos/Newscom, 42; China Photos/Reuters/Corbis, 44

Editor: Thomas K. Adamson
Series Designer: Becky Daum

Library of Congress Control Number: 2014944199

Cataloging-in-Publication Data
Monnig, Alex.
 Aikido / Alex Monnig.
   p. cm. – (Inside martial arts)
ISBN 978-1-62403-601-9 (lib. bdg.)
Includes bibliographical references and index.
1. Aikido–Juvenile literature.   I. Title.
796.815/4–dc23

2014944199

TABLE OF CONTENTS

CHAPTER 1

AIKIDO IN ACTION

A small old man is walking by himself in the park one autumn day. Suddenly two robbers start attacking him. The man's life is on the line.

One of the attackers looks like a professional wrestler. He weighs about 300 pounds. The other is a lightning-quick martial arts expert.

Aikido uses wrist locks for self-defense. This move throws an attacker off balance.

The wrestler charges the old man. The giant grabs the front of his shirt with two strong hands. The old man stays calm. He is an aikido expert. The thugs have picked the wrong target today.

The old man reaches one arm straight up. It goes between the wrestler's arms. The aikido expert bends to his side, as if he is reaching for the wrestler's hip with his free arm.

This makes the big wrestler bend to the side. He is now off balance. The old man flips the wrestler to the ground.

But the danger is not over. The martial arts expert moves in a flash. His fists are so fast they are a blur. The old man dodges the punches.

The attacker tries a spinning kick. The calm old man knows it is coming. His aikido training has given him laser focus. It is almost as if he can read the future. He ducks under the foot. At the same time he grabs the back of the attacker's jacket and yanks him to the ground.

The two attackers come at the old man together now. The martial arts expert tries to punch again. The old man catches one of his arms. He uses the martial artist as a shield by pushing him into the wrestler.

The two attackers are now a jumbled mess. They are confused. The old man moves like a ghost. They cannot get a clean shot on him.

He twists the martial artist's arm backward and down. The attacker has no choice but to fall to the ground in pain.

The giant wrestler gives up. The attackers do not understand why their strength and speed did not work. The old man was always one step ahead.

WHAT DOES IT MEAN?

The word *aikido* has several translations. They all involve balance and harmony. Two of them are "the way of harmonizing energies" and "the way of the harmonious spirit." The "do" in aikido is the part that means "the way." Aikido is about finding harmony every day, not only when doing aikido.

Aikido is not about being able to do flashy moves. It is about finding peace and harmony and using them to help you. People who use aikido are called aikidoka. Aikidoka have a close relationship with nature and the universe. That peace and their training help keep them calm.

Aikido probably began more than 1,000 years ago in Japan. The Minamoto family started a martial arts style called *Daito-ryu Aiki-jujutsu*. They kept it a secret for hundreds of years.

Sokaku Takeda taught this style to Morihei Ueshiba in the early 1900s. Ueshiba is known as the father of modern aikido. He added to Daito-ryu Aiki-jujutsu. Ueshiba combined it with what he knew about nature to create what is now known as aikido. Aikido is more than a way for people to fight and protect themselves. It is also a way to live.

Two aikidoka practice a throw in front of a portrait of Morihei Ueshiba, the inventor of aikido.

CHAPTER 2
TECHNIQUES AND MOVES

Some think aikido is just like karate, jiujitsu, and kung fu. Those martial arts styles are full of punches and kicks. They are shown in the movies.

Aikido is different. Aikidoka use other peoples' movement against them. Aikidoka harmonize with the attackers'

Aikido uses throws to put an attacker on the ground.

Knee walking, or shikko, is a beginning aikido technique.

movements. That is why aikido is a good option for people who are not very strong.

Not all moves are about defeating an attacker. Aikido is about defense. The first thing aikido beginners learn is how to get away from danger. They learn how to roll away from attacks safely. The goal is actually to not have to use self-defense skills.

One of these simple moves is *shikko*. It is sometimes called knee walking. It starts by resting on one knee with the other out in front. Aikidoka slide their feet out from behind them one at a time, switching knees. But they do not actually stand. Trained aikidoka are so smooth they can twirl and glide freely. They move as if they are walking normally. But they are crouched down in a defensive position. They can avoid danger quicker by staying low and not having to be all the way up on their feet.

Attackers sometimes get too close. That means aikidoka are forced into action. The movements are small. But they get the job done.

The key moves in aikido are throws, locks, and pins. Moves are often combined to make a single move. The different kinds of moves are called *waza*. There are hundreds of different waza to learn and master. The most basic moves do not require much strength. But they do take a lot of practice.

Locks can force the trapped person to move in ways the person does not want to. Locks use peoples' joints against them. Joints are places in the body where two or more bones meet, such as the knee or elbow. Locks put pressure on the joints.

It can be very painful when joints are forced to bend or twist backward. The pain forces attackers to move their body to take away the pressure. A simple bending of the hand, arm, or leg can cause even the strongest attackers to crumble. Locks do not always cause pain. Locks can make a series of joints unable to move. This puts the attackers off balance.

A wrist lock can twist the joint in a painful way.

One of the most common types of lock is called a wrist lock. It is a defensive move. An attacker may try to use his or her hands to hit or grab the aikidoka. The aikidoka grabs control of a wrist and twists it into an uncomfortable position in one smooth motion. That makes the attacker bend and become unbalanced. Now it is easier to take the attacker down.

There are several different types of wrist locks. They vary based on where the attack comes from and which way the wrist is locked. Other locks involve arms, fingers, and legs. By twisting a tiny part of the body, an aikidoka can take control of a dangerous situation.

One type of wrist lock is called *tenkai kote hineri*. An attacker comes toward the aikidoka from the front. The aikidoka grabs the attacker's hand and turns the attacker sideways and off balance. The aikidoka then swings the arm back and goes under it. Now the attacker and the aikidoka are facing straight and are side by side. The aikidoka turns to face the attacker and brings the arm down, twisting and locking the wrist. The pressure forces the attacker to bend down helplessly at the waist.

Throws are also important. An example is the *katate dori kokyu nage*. This move allows an aikidoka to defend when an attacker grabs an arm from the front. That attacker's

**An aikidoka throws her opponent during
an aikido demonstration.**

balance is moving forward during the grab. The aikidoka

uses that as an advantage and pulls in the arm.

The pull forces the attacker to stumble and bend forward

at the waist. The aikidoka then shoots an arm up under the

attacker's chin and pushes. This causes the attacker to fall

backward. With only a couple of simple arm movements, the

aikidoka is in control.

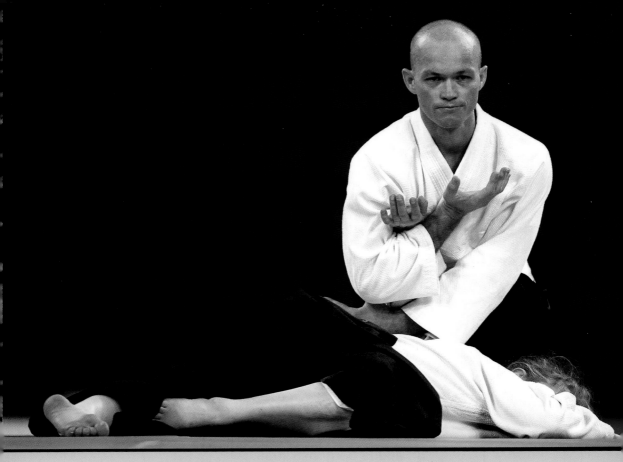

Aikidoka demonstrate how a lock and a pin are good aikido techniques for self-defense.

The aikidoka can then pin the attacker on the ground. Pinning puts pressure on a certain part of the body, such as the shoulder or neck, by twisting or squeezing a joint or nerve.

In the *nikyo* pin, the aikidoka grabs the attacker's hand and twists the arm. This move forces the attacker to the ground to avoid having the arm break. The aikidoka holds on to the arm, twisting it further and pushing the attacker flat onto the ground. The aikidoka then goes to the ground, placing the knee closest to the opponent on the ground up against the armpit. Finally, the aikidoka swings the other knee around to the attacker's head, twisting the attacker's arm further. The fallen predator now has no way to escape.

AIKIDO MOVES

Wrist Lock

This move forces an attacker to stop moving for fear of the wrist breaking. A wrist lock is a common defense from grabs. It can immobilize an attacker when performed correctly.

Tenkai Kote Hineri

This wrist lock forces the attacker to bend down helplessly at the waist.

Nikyo Pin

Pins immobilize an attacker in a harmless position, unable to move or attack. This lets aikidoka remain in control of attackers before deciding what to do next.

Kote Gaeshi

This throw starts by taking control of an attacker's wrist and turning it out. The aikidoka then uses the attacker's momentum to spin them through the air and plant them on the ground.

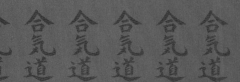

CHAPTER 3
TRAINING

Most aikido training takes place in dojos. The dojo is the training ground for aikido. Aikido is an art. No artist or piece of art is exactly the same. It is the same with aikido dojos.

Dojos can be any place where students gather to learn the art of aikido. Some buildings are created only for people to learn aikido. A dojo can

An aikido teacher shows a student how to do a wrist lock in a dojo.

also be a room used for teaching in a school or gym filled with mats.

Dojos are run by teachers who have years of experience in aikido. Teachers are aikidoka who have spent decades studying aikido. Teachers will say they know very little about aikido compared with how much there is to know.

Often teachers have tiny differences in the way they train students. Some teachers add their own unique style to the aikido that Sensei Morihei Ueshiba brought to the world. Different styles are taught in different parts of the world.

ALL ABOUT AIKIDO

The Aikikai Foundation was created by the Japanese government in 1940. It helps increase interest and participation in aikido throughout the world. It sets up aikido schools and writes books and newspapers about the art. The group's headquarters is still in Tokyo, Japan.

Aikidoka learn their techniques in a dojo.

Aikidoka train for hours in a dojo to become stronger and more flexible.

Grading aikidoka can also be different. Some martial arts use belts to show how much people have learned. Many aikido masters do this, too. But the ranking system can change between dojos.

Kyu and *dan* are the two main types of aikido ranks. Beginning ranks are called kyu. Some dojos, particularly in the United States, have different colored belts for kyu ranks.

After finishing kyu stages, it is time for the black belt. Black

belt stages are called dan.

The aikido gi is loose fitting to make it easier
for aikidoka to move during training.

Students train for many hours before earning their next belt. When a student and a teacher believe the time is right, students perform a specific series of moves to prove they are ready to move to the next level. The students need to do the moves smoothly without hesitation. They also show they understand the harmony and balance of aikido.

An aikido uniform is called a *gi*. The pants are baggy. The knees have extra layers of fabric for knee walking and doing techniques from the kneeling position. The top is like a robe with a belt around the waist. Aikido gis have short sleeves. That makes it easier for students to practice wrist locks. The loose clothing lets aikidoka move freely while practicing moves.

Aikido training is very controlled. Students do not attack each other without a plan. Instead, they take turns playing roles. It is as if they are actors practicing a play. The person playing the role of the attacker is called a *uke*. Ukes do

The techniques aikidoka learn are controlled. They practice carefully so that they learn the moves properly.

not use aikido on the sparring partner. The person being attacked and who does the aikido move is called the *tori*.

The uke's attacks on the tori are usually planned. That way the tori can practice more. *Jiyu waza* is a free-form practice. The uke chooses how to attack, and the tori has to respond. Aikidoka learn through careful practice.

Nobody learns every single thing Sensei Morihei Ueshiba knew about aikido. But the longer somebody practices, the better that person gets. This is easy to see with aikidoka who have more experience. They do not have to think about the moves they do. The moves flow out of them naturally. It is as if they are connected to aikido on a different level.

HARMONY

Harmony is another name for balance. It is maybe the most important thing to know about aikido. Most throws and locks in aikido are about keeping attackers unbalanced. That is why aikidoka need to stay in control of their own bodies. Harmony is important not only on the outside. It is also important on the inside. Sensei Morihei Ueshiba believed learning aikido connects people to the universe. Living like that helps separate kyu from dan.

Aikido is more than simply being able to perform all the different moves. It is also a way of life. It takes years to become an expert in the moves and the lifestyle.

The uke and tori practice their attacks and defenses only with careful plans.

CHAPTER 4

ADVANCED AIKIDO

Becoming an aikido expert takes thousands of hours of training. Most dojos require two to three years of training between each dan stage. There are usually about eight to 10 dan stages, although it can vary in different styles and dojos. But mastering aikido takes more than only going to class and learning moves. Students

Aikidoka train for years before earning a black belt and each dan stage.

need to work hard on their skills in and out of the dojo.

Much of aikido is about harmony with other people and things. This is something that aikidoka can always improve. In a way, aikidoka are always training. The way they behave in normal situations can help with balance and harmony. Aikido experts can connect their bodies, minds, and souls into one flowing movement.

The old man who was attacked in the park showed these skills. He was so calm and balanced that it was as if he could read the future. His aikido training taught him to tune out distractions. He controlled his feelings and thoughts. He focused only on defending himself. Aikido does

Advanced aikidoka calmly practice their moves to perfection.

not give people superpowers. But it can make it seem that way to attackers.

Having the right attitude is important for both the uke and the tori. If a uke does not try hard in attack, then the

Aikido throws are not flashy. Aikidoka throw the attacker to the ground as quickly as possible.

tori will not learn how to do the move correctly. That means he or she will not be prepared to survive a real attack.

Advanced aikidoka know that the art is not about looking cool. Throws are done to be as useful as possible. Gravity is an aikidoka's friend. Aikidoka get attackers down to the ground and in control as soon as possible. Moves flow smoothly. But the moves are not designed for show.

Aikidoka learn more complicated moves as they train more. At first the moves can be pretty simple. Many moves involve a lock and pushing or grabbing an attacker. Those

Advanced aikidoka learn how to defend against attacks with weapons. The uke is using a fake knife for this practice.

Advanced aikidoka also learn to defend against sword attacks.

moves are usually enough to do the job. Some aikidoka like to challenge themselves.

For advanced aikidoka, training can become dangerous. Those students have to do moves against attackers with weapons. Besides throws and locks, dan have to prove they can disarm foes. Some examples of these moves are called *tanto dori* (knife takeaway) and *tachi dori* (sword takeaway).

Advanced aikidoka can also deal with multiple attackers coming at them at the same time. The old man in the park shows how to do this. It is hard to defend against more than one person. An aikidoka will use one attacker as a weapon against the others. Aikidoka move quickly to surprise the attackers. They want to be in places the attackers do not expect.

As aikidoka move up the dan ranks, they can learn how to disarm every attacker.

CHAPTER 5

TRAINING FOR ONESELF

Most types of martial arts styles have competitions. Fighters will sometimes travel around the world to go head to head. The winners get trophies and other prizes.

Aikido generally does not have meets or competitions. Competing goes against what aikido is about. Aikido is a personal art. It teaches students to become better people. Trying to injure

Aikidoka promote aikido at demonstrations all over the world, like at this one in Beijing, China.

another person to win a contest is not in line with those beliefs. Instead, aikidoka focus on getting better. There are no prizes for the best students. All aikido students have to think about is learning the technique. This helps it become a way of life.

The exception is a style called *shodokan*, or *Tomiki* aikido. Sensei Tomiki started it. He was a level eight dan in both judo and aikido. Tomiki learned from Sensei Jigoro Kano. Kano founded modern-day judo. Tomiki also learned from Sensei Morihei Ueshiba, who founded aikido.

Tomiki invented his style using parts of both aikido and judo. One element he took from judo was the idea of competition. Tomiki did think aikido was about harmony. He agreed that being in touch with oneself and the universe was important.

He also thought that attacks in real life are more dangerous than dojo training. So Tomiki started competitions

Jigoro Kano developed judo in the late 1800s.

Some aikidoka use competitions to train for real-life attacks.

to help people train for those real-life attacks. In some of the contests, people do moves against somebody attacking them with a fake knife.

The Aikido World Championships happen every two years. The championships have many different events based on rank and gender. Competitors are judged on how smoothly they can execute the moves. Some of the events involve defending against fake knife attacks.

Tomiki thinks competition is the best way to prepare for actual dangerous situations. But many aikidoka around the world disagree. They say it encourages people to focus on harming each other with aikido. They say competition is not harmony.

Many people enjoy the competition style of aikido. That is what makes the art so great. Everyone's behavior and attitude are different. Aikido can mean different things to different people. For all aikidoka, it is an exciting and fun way to live a happier life.

GLOSSARY

aikidoka
Somebody who practices aikido.

dan
The advanced ranks of aikido that include black belts.

dojo
A place where people learn aikido.

harmony
Being in agreement.

kyu
The beginning ranks of aikido that can include white or multicolored belts.

lock
Gaining control of a limb, most likely a part of the arm or leg, by grabbing and twisting.

sensei
An experienced martial arts teacher.

uke
The attacking person in aikido training.

waza
An aikido move.

FOR MORE INFORMATION

Further Readings

Brady, Peter. *Aikido: Step By Step*. Leicester, UK: Lorenz, 2013.

Saotome, Mitsugi. *Aikido and the Harmony of Nature*. Boston, MA: Shambhala, 2013.

Shiodo, Gozo and Yasuhisa Shiodo. *Aikido: The Complete Basic Techniques*. New York: Kodansha USA, 2013.

Shiodo, Gozo. *Dynamic Aikido*. New York: Kodansha USA, 2013.

Websites

To learn more about Inside Martial Arts, visit **booklinks.abdopublishing.com**. These links are routinely monitored and updated to provide the most current information available.

INDEX

ABOUT THE AUTHOR

Alex Monnig is a freelance journalist from Saint Louis, Missouri, who now lives in Sydney, Australia. He graduated with his master's degree from the University of Missouri in May 2010. During his career he has spent time covering sporting events around the world, including the 2008 Olympic Games in China, the 2010 Commonwealth Games in India, the 2011 Rugby World Cup in New Zealand, and the 2014 Olympic Winter Games in Russia.